HERstory

HERstory

A young women's journey of self-discovery through creative writing and dynamic interactive activities

Student Writing Companion

GIRL FRIDAY BOOKS

Copyright © 2022 The Leadership Program

All rights reserved.

No part of this book may be reproduced, or stored in a retrieval system, or transmitted in any form or by any means, electronic, mechanical, photocopying, recording, or otherwise, without express written permission of the publisher.

Created by The Leadership Program, New York
www.theleadershipprogram.com

The Leadership Program
535 8th Avenue, Floor 16
New York, NY 10018

Published by Girl Friday Books™, Seattle
www.girlfridaybooks.com

Produced by Girl Friday Productions

ISBN 978-1-959411-03-1

Printed in the United States of America

Welcome to HERstory! In this workbook you will have the opportunity to express your thoughts, feelings, and opinions about issues that are relevant to your life today and to your dreams for the future. These pages offer an assortment of activities and opportunities to write about yourself and the world in diverse formats. Enjoy the journey.

THIS BOOK BELONGS TO . . .

Contents

1. Community Building

Guess Who I Am
- A "Me" Inventory 2

R.E.S.P.E.C.T.
- Respect Yourself! 3

Human Spectrum
- Diversity Pursuit 4

The Ties That Bind
- My Life 5
- Mountains and Valleys 6
- Your Many Roles 7

Lights, Camera, Action!
- Get It While It's Hot! 8
- Can't Use It? Just Sell It! 9

Introduction to Character
- Character Worksheet 10
- Your Top Ten Character Qualities 11
- Character Profile 12
- Why I Am the Way I Am 14
- Personality Goes a Long Way 16

Ethical Minds Want to Know
- Ethical Case Study 18
- Questionable Ethics 20
- Ethical Minds Want to Know 21

Personal Values Posters
- Match the Value 23
- Value Wheel 24

Choices, Decisions, Consequences
- Choices, Decisions, Consequences Sample Model 27
- Choices, Decisions, Consequences: Setting the Scene 28
- Choices, Decisions, Consequences Role Play 29
- Decisions 30

Free Your Voice
- Movie Response Questions: *Freedom Writers* 31

❷ Writing Workshop

Who's the Woman?
- Who's the Woman? 34
- Lyric Breakdown 35
- Writing Workshop Part One: Identity 36
- I Am . . . Poem 39
- Final I Am . . . Poem 40
- Hold On . . . Poem 41
- Final Hold On . . . Poem 42
- Reflection Poem 43
- Final Reflection Poem 44
- Movie Response Questions: *13 Going On 30* 45

Lean on Me
- My Inner Circle 47
- Who Can I Turn To? 48
- Lean on Me 49
- Writing Workshop Part Two: Those You Are Closest To 50
- Movie Response Questions: *The Sisterhood of the Traveling Pants* 56

Body Positive!
- Get Plump 58
- Body Intelligence 59
- Body Appreciation 61
- Writing Workshop Part Three: Body Image 62
- Movie Response Questions: *Real Women Have Curves* 65

Make a Connection
- Create Your Own Personals Ad 67
- Rate Your Mate 68
- Writing Workshop Part Four: Love and Relationships 69
- Movie Response Questions: *Enchanted* 72

Great Expectations!
- For Just One Day 74
- Great Expectations! 75
- Writing Workshop Part Five: Dreams 76
- Movie Response Questions: *Take the Lead* 78

Around My Way
- Around My Way 80
- Show Your Pride 82
- Writing Workshop Part Six: Heritage or Tradition 83
- I Am from . . . Poem 85
- Final I Am from . . . Poem 87
- Movie Response Questions: *The Great Debaters* 88

The Road Less Traveled
- Imagine 90
- The Road Not Taken 92
- Map of Your Dreams 93
- Writing Workshop Part Seven: Legacy 94
- Movie Response Questions: *Pay It Forward* 96

3 Creative Output

What's Our Style?
- Group Poem 100

What Do I Stand For?
- Collage Poem 101

Literary Journal: The Art of Words
- The Art of Words Guide 102

Introduction to Acting
- Say More: Journal Exercise 116

Credits 118

About The Leadership Program 119

Community Building

1

"The good we secure for ourselves is precarious and uncertain until it is secured for all of us and incorporated into our common life."
—Jane Addams

"I know there is strength in the differences between us. I know there is comfort, where we overlap." —Ani DiFranco

A "Me" Inventory

THREE THINGS I DO EXTREMELY WELL: 1. 2. 3.	THREE THINGS I DO OKAY: 1. 2. 3.	THREE THINGS I DO, BUT WOULD BE EXTREMELY HAPPY NEVER TO DO AGAIN: 1. 2. 3.
THREE THINGS ABOUT MYSELF THAT I REALLY LIKE: 1. 2. 3.	THREE THINGS ABOUT MYSELF THAT ARE OKAY: 1. 2. 3.	THREE THINGS ABOUT MYSELF THAT I WISH I COULD CHANGE: 1. 2. 3.
THREE GOOD THINGS OTHER PEOPLE THINK ABOUT ME: 1. 2. 3.	THREE THINGS THAT OTHER PEOPLE THINK ABOUT ME THAT ARE OKAY: 1. 2. 3.	THREE THINGS THAT I WISH OTHER PEOPLE DIDN'T THINK ABOUT ME: 1. 2. 3.

 Bonus: After filling out the grid, put a star next to all the items that you can control (e.g., I'm a good friend). Put a zero next to all the items you can't control (e.g., I like the color of my eyes).

Respect Yourself!

1. Choose one of the ways to respect yourself that came up in the game today that you do *not* already do and that you can commit to doing between now and the next HERstory session. Write it below.

   One way I will respect myself is by _____
   _____

2. What do you think it will be like to respect yourself in this way?
   _____

3. Do you think you can commit to respecting yourself in this way on a regular basis? Why or why not?
   _____

4. What are three things you already do in your life to respect yourself?
   1. _____
   2. _____
   3. _____

5. What are three things you don't do but would like to do to respect yourself?
   1. _____
   2. _____
   3. _____

6. What do you feel is the main thing that gets in the way of you respecting yourself?
   _____

Diversity Pursuit

Has a family member with a disability	Has witnessed others being bullied because they were perceived as being different	Speaks more than one language	Listens to the same type of music you do	Believes that all people are created equal
Has more than one race or culture in her family	Has read a book about a group of people different from herself	Has assisted someone with a disability	Has a friend or family member in the military	Wears clothing unique to her culture
Has a close friend of the opposite gender	Has a name with religious or cultural significance	Has ever been treated differently because of the way she looks	Has spoken up when someone said "that's so gay," "that's retarded," or another offensive term	Has traveled to another country
Is an only child	Celebrates holidays that are different from yours	Has a Facebook friend in another country	Went to a religious school	Was born in another country
Has experienced discrimination	Has attended the Puerto Rican Day parade	Has volunteered at a homeless shelter or soup kitchen	Knows sign language	Doesn't judge people by their sexual orientation

My Life

Life is full of highs and lows. Sometimes we have mountains, and sometimes valleys.

Think about your life and what you consider to be your biggest highs and lows so far, then write about them in the space below.

MOUNTAINS	VALLEYS

HERstory | 5

Mountains and Valleys

Has ever won an award	Has ever lost a pet	Has ever made another person feel good about himself/herself	Has ever felt guilty	Has ever insulted someone
Has ever felt afraid	Has ever been broken up with by a boyfriend or girlfriend	Has ever done really well on an important test	Has ever felt excited about something	Has ever had a loved one pass away
Has ever been called a racial slur	Has ever been accused of something	Has ever felt alone	Has ever fallen in love	Has ever felt completely happy
Has ever been judged by someone	Has ever done well at a sport or hobby	Has ever been pleasantly surprised	Has ever discovered something new about herself	Has ever been given an unexpected gift
Has ever felt embarrassed	Has ever had something stolen	Has ever made a team or a program that she really wanted to be part of	Has ever made a mistake	Has ever been proud of herself

Your Many Roles

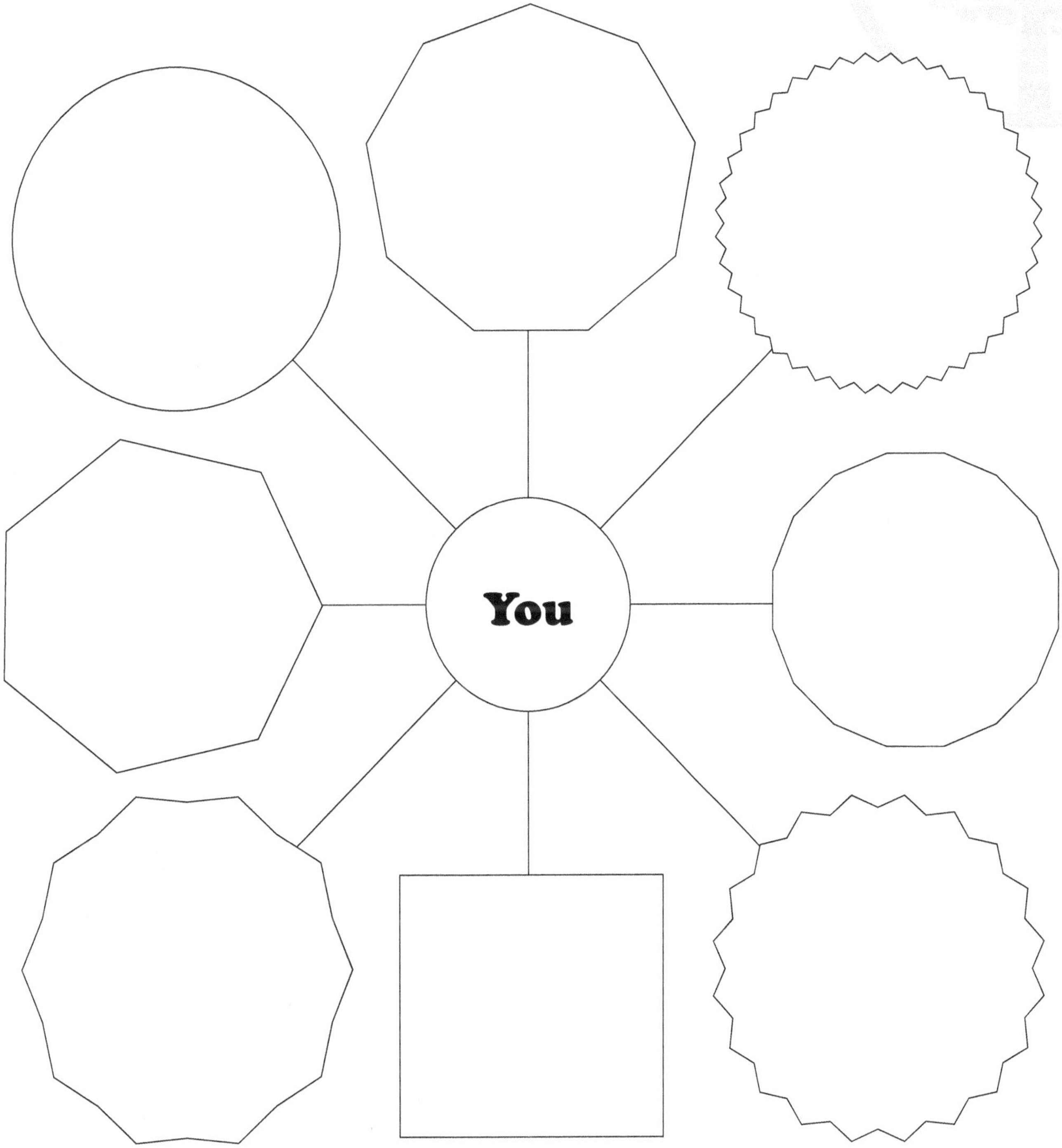

You

HERstory | 7

Get It While It's Hot!

Write an ad for a hard-to-sell product in the space below.

Be as creative and detailed as possible.

Can't Use It? Just Sell It!

Instructions

- Your task as a team is to create a commercial for a hard-to-sell product (e.g., a bucket with no bottom).

- Brainstorm as many selling points as possible about your product and include a demonstration of how to use it. Try to think of all the reasons why someone in your target audience should buy this product.

- Promote this hard-to-sell product to *two* separate target audiences (noted on your index card) by creating two different commercials, one for each target audience.

- Use as many props from your prop bag as possible in your commercials.

- Be as creative as you can!

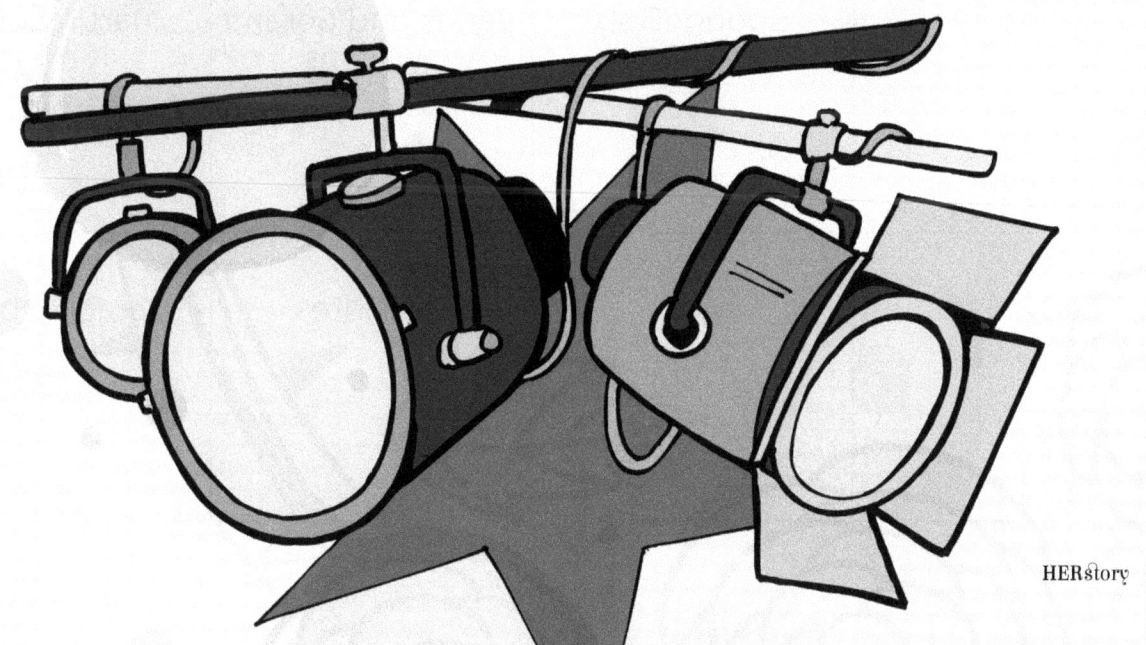

Character Worksheet

Grandmothers	Victor Cruz		Lil Wayne
	minister	Angelina Jolie	George W. Bush
Michelle Obama	Jay-Z	Hillary Clinton	teachers
	SpongeBob SquarePants	Venus and Serena Williams	Martin Luther King Jr.
Lady Gaga		Bill Gates	Barack Obama

Your Top Ten Character Qualities

List Your Qualities:

1.

2.

3.

4.

5.

6.

7.

8.

9.

10.

Reorganize Your List in Order of Importance to You:

1.

2.

3.

4.

5.

6.

7.

8.

9.

10.

Character Profile

A PERSON WHOSE CHARACTER HAS IMPRESSED YOU:
_____

(Answer the questions below according to what you know and what you would suppose about this person. *If you don't know, guess.*)

1. One quality of this person's character that has affected me:

2. One example of how that character quality affected me:

3. One thing this person has said that I can remember:

4. How do other people see this person? (*As a . . .*)

5. Who or what do I think shaped this person's character?

6. How do I see this person motivating himself/herself? (What seems to make him/her want to make an effort and do things?)

7. If there was one thing this person would want to pass on as his/her legacy to others, what do I think it would be?

8. What parts of the person's character have I seen him/her work to improve?

Choose two of the questions above and answer them *about yourself* in the two spaces below:

1.

2.

Why I Am the Way I Am

You are who you choose to be, but your personality—what makes you *you*—comes from traits you're born with and traits you've picked up from the world around you. Personality goes a long way. What's yours?

PART 1

In the space below, list some of the parts of your personality that are specific and peculiar to you (e.g., your sense of humor, the way your mind works, your sense of style).

PART 2

Looking at some of the traits you just wrote down, think about where these aspects of your personality and the character traits we discussed earlier may have come from.

In the space below, divide each of your personality and character traits into one of the following two categories: **Born with It** (e.g., traits your family gave you) and **Picked It Up** (e.g., what you've adopted from your neighborhood, your school, your community, television, movies, fashion).

THE WAY I AM

Born with It:

Picked It Up:

Personality Goes a Long Way

PART 1

Some personality or character traits you're born with. Some you pick up along the way. Fill in the columns below to rate the traits of your personality and character—which traits you like, which you wish you could change, and where you think they came from.

PERSONALITY/CHARACTER TRAITS I LIKE ABOUT MYSELF:	WHERE I THINK THEY CAME FROM:
1.	
2.	
3.	
4.	
5.	

PERSONALITY/CHARACTER TRAITS I WISH I COULD CHANGE ABOUT MYSELF:	WHERE I THINK THEY CAME FROM:
1.	
2.	
3.	
4.	
5.	

PART 2

1. How can you maintain the personality/character traits you like about yourself?

2. How can you change the personality/character traits you don't like about yourself?

Ethical Case Study

Read the following case study and answer the questions that follow.

Several years ago, a librarian was working the reference desk at the public library in her community. The phone rang. The caller, a male, wanted some information on state laws concerning assault. The librarian asked several questions to clarify the nature of his inquiry. Then, in keeping with long-established library policy designed to keep phone lines from being tied up, she explained that she would call him back in a few minutes after researching his question. She took down his first name and phone number, and then hung up.

The librarian was just getting up to do the research when a man who had been sitting in the reading area within earshot of the reference desk approached her. Flashing a police detective's badge, he asked for the name and number of the caller. The reason: the conversation he had overheard led him to suspect that the caller was the perpetrator of an assault that had happened the night before in the community.

What should the librarian have done? On one hand, she was a member of the community. She felt very strongly about the need to maintain law and order. As a woman, she was particularly concerned that an attacker might be at large in the community. And as a citizen, she wanted to do whatever she could to reduce the possibility that he might strike again. After all, what if she refused to tell and another assault happened the following night?

On the other hand, she felt just as strongly that her professional code as a librarian required her to protect the confidentiality of *all* callers. She felt that free access to information was vital to the success of democracy, and that if people seeking information were being watched and categorized simply by the kinds of questions they asked, a police state was not far behind. The right of privacy, she felt, must extend to everyone. After all, what if this caller was simply a student writing a paper on assault laws for a civics class?

The choice the librarian faced was clearly a difficult one. It was right to support the community's quest for law and order. But it was also right to honor confidentiality, as her professional code required.

Ethical Case Study Questions

1. What two groups was the librarian a part of that defined her ethics?

2. What were those ethics?

3. Describe why the ethics are in conflict.

4. If you were in this situation, what would you do?

Questionable Ethics

Choose one of the following questions to answer. Explain why you would make your decision and include what ethics come into play in making your decision.

- Would you commit a crime and spend a year in maximum-security prison if it meant that when you got out you'd be guaranteed $1 million?

- You really want a new iPad. Would you take one from a friend who admitted that he broke into a house, beat up the owner, and stole the iPad last weekend?

- Would you lie under oath in a court of law and say you witnessed a cop beat up an African American man in your neighborhood? What you actually saw was the cop push the man, not beat him up. However, you feel that so many cops get away with brutality, so why not try to make this cop an example?

....
....
....
....
....
....
....
....
....
....

Ethical Minds Want to Know

Part One

What are four groups to which you belong?
Example: Sports team, family, religious congregation

1.	3.
2.	4.

Part Two

Fill in your four groups in the spaces provided at the top of each column. Write some of the ethics of that group in the boxes provided underneath. **Circle** the ethics that you feel are easy for you to follow. **Underline** the ethics that you feel are harder to follow.

Group:	Group:	Group:	Group:

Ethical Minds Want to Know

Part Three

Base all of your answers on the ethics that you identified on the previous page.

1. Which ethics are easy for you to follow?

2. Which ethics are harder for you to follow?

3. Are there any ethics you don't necessarily agree with but follow because you are a part of that group? Why?

4. How do the ethics of these groups affect who you are?

Match the Value

Connect the leader with one value he or she lives/lived by.

Nelson Mandela   Nonviolence

Gandhi   "Any man or institution that tries to rob me of my dignity will lose."

Jackie Robinson   "By any means necessary."

Mother Teresa   Equality

Martin Luther King Jr.   "I'm free to be *me*!"

Muhammad Ali   Love and service

Malcolm X   Turn the other cheek

Value Wheel

Part One

Prioritize each category by numbering each section of the wheel according to what you value most in your life (1 denotes the most important).

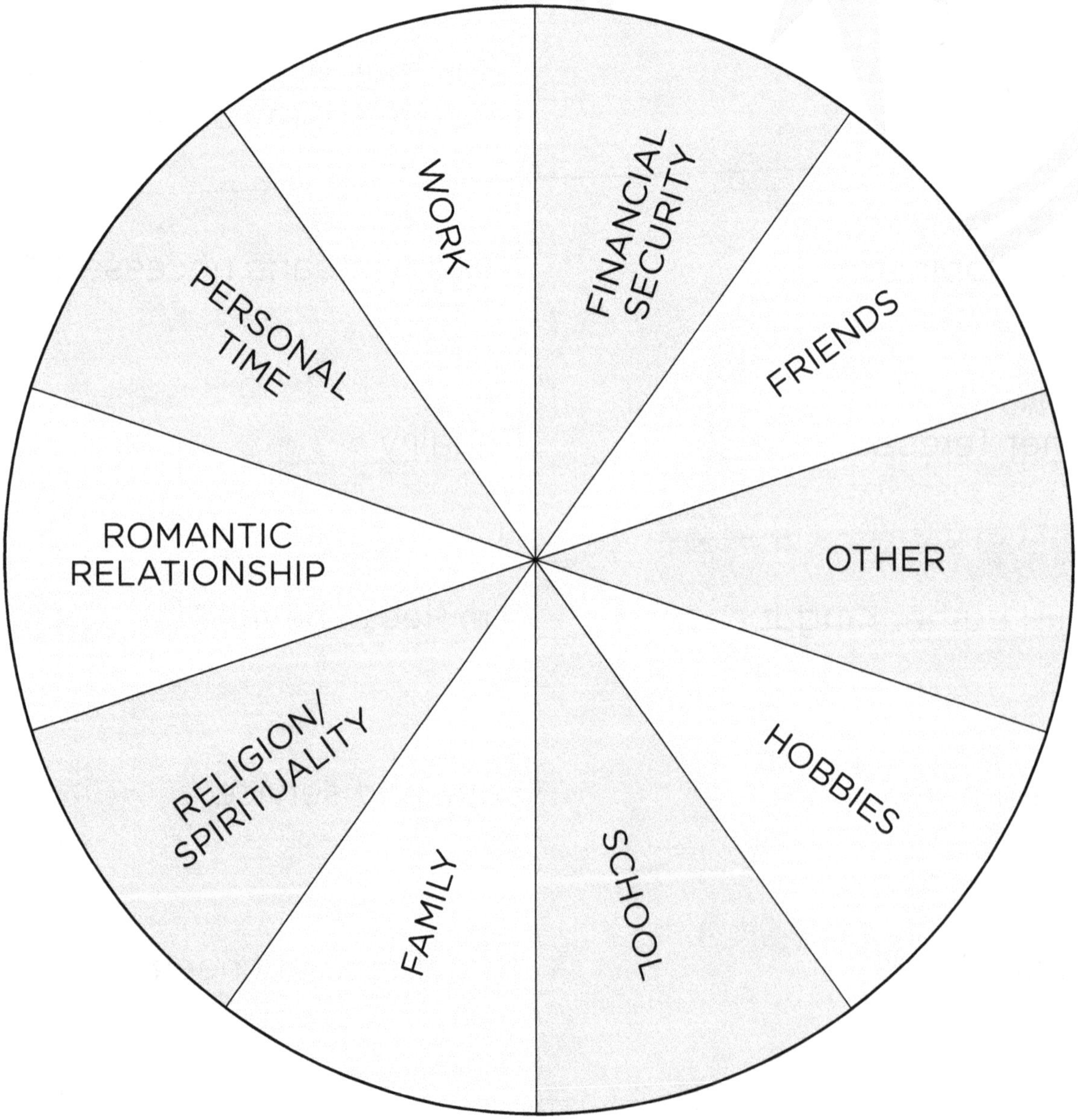

Wheel sections: WORK, FINANCIAL SECURITY, FRIENDS, OTHER, HOBBIES, SCHOOL, FAMILY, RELIGION/SPIRITUALITY, ROMANTIC RELATIONSHIP, PERSONAL TIME

Value Wheel

Part Two

List the top four categories that you value most from your wheel. Think about why each category is a priority in your life and what about it is most important to you. For each category create a personal value statement.

Category	Personal Value Statement
Example: Work	Work is necessary for success.
Example: Family	Blood is thicker than water.

1. _____   _____

2. _____   _____

3. _____   _____

4. _____   _____

Value Wheel

Part Three

Answer the following questions.

1. If you became famous, what is one thing you'd want the world to know about the "real" you?

   ....
   ....
   ....
   ....

2. If you were to write your future grandchild a letter, what would you tell him/her is one of the most important things to know in life?

   ....
   ....
   ....
   ....

3. Who is someone whom you consider a personal role model? What is one value that he/she lives by that is also important to you?

   ....
   ....
   ....
   ....

Choices, Decisions, Consequences

Sample Model

Situation: Friends tell you another student has been spreading terrible rumors about you.

Choices	Decisions	Consequences
• Fight • Ignore It • Spread rumors about him or her • Tell a teacher	Fight	• Get hurt • Suspension • Props for being tough
	Ignore it	• Rumors stop • Rumors get worse • Stay in school
	Spread rumors about him or her	• Hurt feelings • Physical violence • Suspension
	Tell a teacher	• Teacher helps stop the rumors • Kids call you a snitch • Your parents find out

Choices, Decisions, Consequences

Setting the Scene

Answer the following questions and write out a situation that can be enacted in class.

Who are the characters in the scene?

Character A:

Character B:

Where will the characters be in the scene?

....
....
....
....

What is the situation?

....
....
....
....
....
....
....
....

Choices, Decisions, Consequences

Role Play

1. Decide what the situation is.
2. Decide who the characters will be.
3. Decide where the scene will take place.
4. List all the choices, decisions, and consequences.
5. Select one decision to be enacted, and circle it.
6. Select one consequence to be enacted, and circle it.
7. Decide who will play character A and character B in the scene. Only two people should be acting in the scene. The others in the group may introduce the scene, direct it, freeze it, etcetera.
8. Rehearse the scene.

1. Situation:

2. Character A: Character B:

3. Where will the scene take place?

4.

Choices	Decisions	Consequences

HERstory | 29

Decisions

Select a real-life situation in which you have to make an important decision. Complete the choices, decisions, and consequences portion of the chart.

Situation:

....
....
....
....
....
....

Choices	Decisions	Consequences

Movie Response Questions

Freedom Writers

DATE:

1. Why do you think the students in *Freedom Writers* decided to tell their stories?

2. How did it feel to hear these students tell their stories?

3. Do you like to write about things that you think/feel? If so, why? If not, why not?

4. Why is it important to write about your experiences and feelings?

5. What kinds of things can we learn by reading other people's stories?

6. What would you like to teach people through writing your own story?

Writing Workshop

2

"Do not follow where the path may lead. Go instead where there is no path and leave a trail." —Muriel Strode

"Your writing voice is the deepest possible reflection of who you are." —Meg Rosoff

Who's the Woman?

This question has always been
"Who's the man?" but now we've flipped it
and want to know, "Who's the woman?"
What are you expected to do,
what are you forbidden to do,
and what are the rules?
Today we are going to be exploring these issues
thoroughly, most definitely, definitively, through and through.

Please take a moment to complete the following statements to create a list poem. Whatever's clever, but don't take forever.

Part One: Sentence Completion

A woman is _____

A woman feels _____

A woman should _____

A woman cannot _____

A woman must _____

A woman needs _____

A woman wants _____

A woman believes _____

A woman becomes _____

Part Two: Brainstorm

Who's the woman to you?_____

A woman is expected to _____

A woman is forbidden to _____

Lyric Breakdown

1. What do the chosen lyrics have in common? Explain and give an example.

   ....
   ....
   ....

2. How are these lyrics different? Explain and give an example.

   ....
   ....
   ....

3. Choose one song and summarize its message in one sentence.

   ....
   ....
   ....

4. Is there a music artist today who you feel advises or addresses women and how they should be and behave? Give an example.

   ....
   ....
   ....

Writing Workshop Part One

Identity

1. What are three things that you want the world to know about you?

2. How do you think young women should be treated?

3. What is the best thing about being a young woman? What is the worst thing?

4. Do people have expectations of you? If so, what are they?

5. How do you think the world sees you?

6. How do you wish the world saw you?

7. What is something that you think you are good at? Something that you wish you were better at?

8. What do you think is the best part of your personality?

9. What is a part of your personality that you would like to improve?

I Am . . . Poem

Fill in the spaces below with the description in the parentheses.

I am . . .
(Sounds you heard growing up)

....

I am . . .
(Foods you eat)

....

I am . . .
(Names in your family)

....

I am . . .
(Places you lived)

....

I am . . .
(Choose a topic from the box below or create your own: _____)

....

I am . . .
(Choose a topic from the box below or create your own: _____)

....

> TOPICS: music you listen to, magazines you read, hobbies you have, friends you have, family you listen to, things that make you who you are, the communities you live in, subjects you love, issues that matter to you, family traditions, nationalities, games you play, smells from your childhood

HERstory

Final I Am . . . Poem

I am . . .

I am . . .

I am . . .

I am . . .

I am . . .

I am . . .

I am _____

Hold On . . . Poem

Fill in the spaces below with your thoughts on how to complete the sentence.

Hold on . . . even if . . .

Hold on . . . even if . . .

Hold on . . . even if . . .

Hold on . . . even if . . .

Hold on . . . even if . . .

Hold on . . . even if . .

Final Hold On . . . Poem

Hold on . . . even if . . .

Hold on . . . even if . . .

Hold on . . . even if . . .

Hold on . . . even if . . .

Hold on . . . even if . . .

Hold on . . . even if . . .

Reflection Poem

Fill in the spaces below with your thoughts on how to complete the sentences.

I used to think . . .

But now I know . . .

I always thought . . .

But I never . . .

I once felt . . .

But now I see . . .

If I could . . .

I would . . .

I never . . .

But I might . . .

I can't . . .

But I can . . .

I won't . . .

But I might . . .

I used to think . . .

But now I know . . .

Final Reflection Poem

I used to think . . .

But now I know . . .

I always thought . . .

But I never . . .

I once felt . . .

But now I see . . .

If I could . . .

I would . . .

I never . . .

But I might . . .

I can't . . .

But I can . . .

I won't . . .

But I might . . .

I used to think . . .

But now I know . . .

Movie Response Questions

13 Going On 30

1. Jenna's birthday wish is to grow up. What does being grown-up mean to you?

2. There were some elements of Jenna that were completely the same as both her thirteen- and thirty-year-old self. What parts of your character do you want to retain as you get older?

3. When Jenna wakes up as a thirty-year-old she has everything she dreamed of having when she was thirteen, yet she feels like something is missing. What do you think is missing for her? What are some things that you could not be happy without?

4. There is a popular saying that goes "The grass is always greener on the other side." Why do you think people always want what they don't have?

5. Jenna learns about what she really values as she faces certain obstacles throughout the course of the movie. Have you ever had an experience that helped you better understand what you value most?

6. Why is it important to accept **yourself** and **be at peace** with who you are?

My Inner Circle

In the center circle, write the names of the people you consider your closest friends. In the second circle, write the names of the people you like a lot but are not the first ones who you run to with a secret. Then, in the largest circle, write the names of people you just hang out with occasionally or casually. Next to each name, write the role that the person plays in your life.

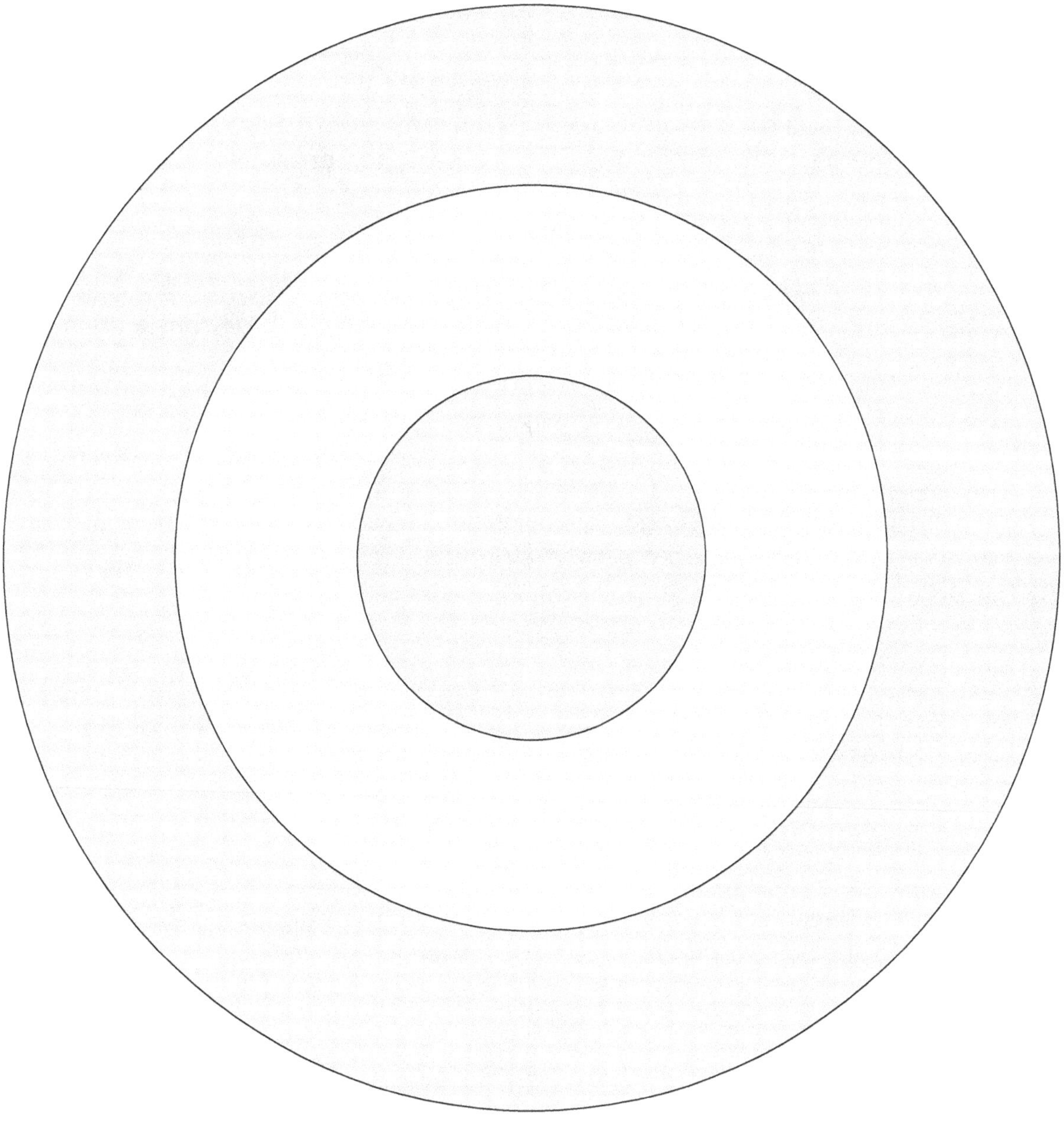

Who Can I Turn To?

In each box, write the role or name of as many people as you can think of to whom you can turn in the situation described.

When my best friend betrays me . . . (e.g., my sister Tamika, another friend)	When I need new clothes for a party and don't have any money . . .
When I don't understand the current math assignment and there's a test tomorrow . . .	When my mom/dad grounds me and there is a party tomorrow night . . .
When I feel as if one of my teachers hates me . . .	If someone in my family has a drinking or drug problem . . .
When I had a fight with someone and now I have a problem with everyone that person hangs out with . . .	When I'm not included in the group of popular kids . . .
When there is a girl/boy I like and I don't know if she/he likes me . . .	When I feel that my parents don't understand me . . .
When I feel torn between school and outside responsibilities or distractions . . .	When I'm not getting along with my brothers or sisters . . .

Lean on Me

Here are your many support systems. Fill in the names of the people in each of your planets.

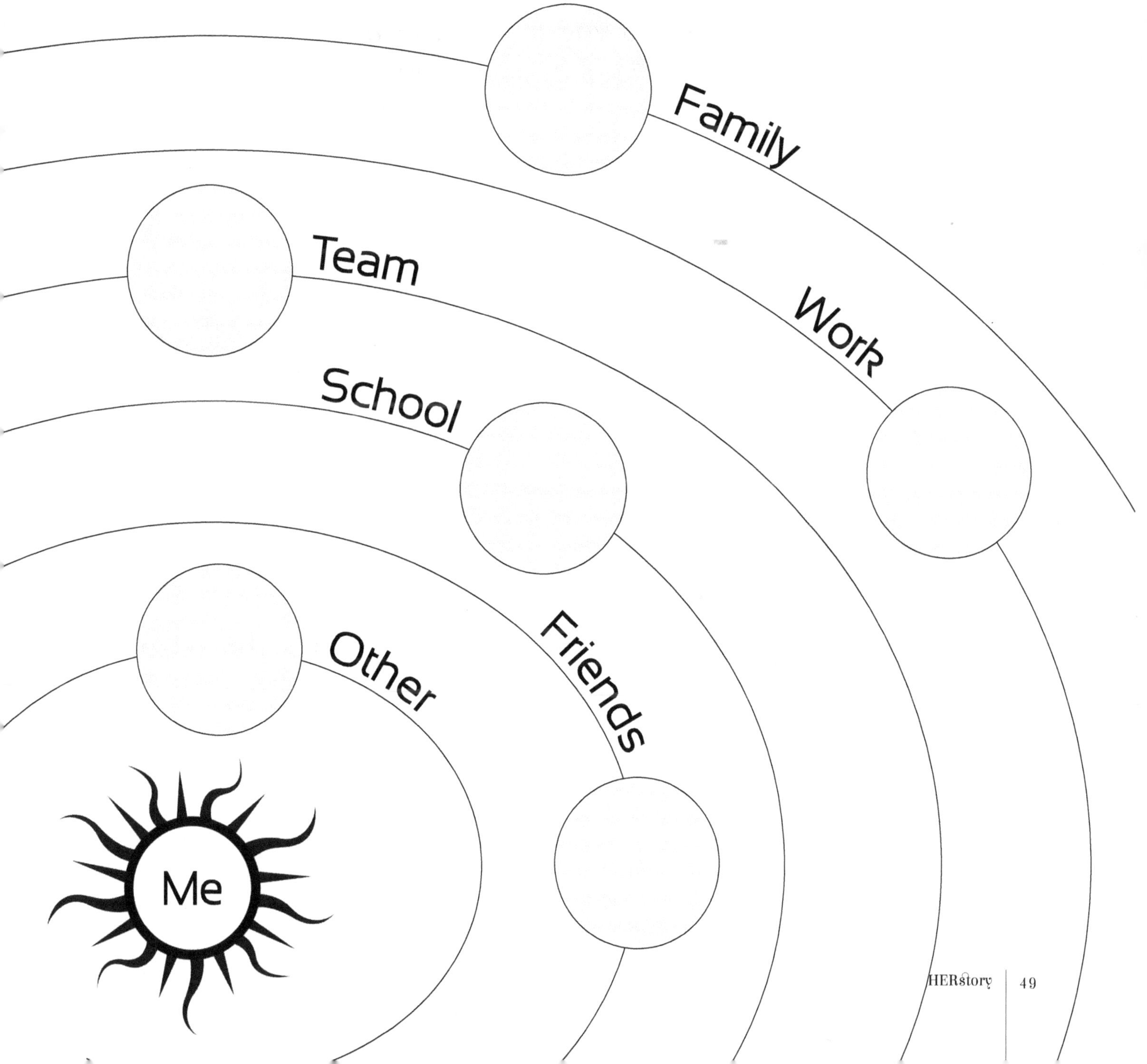

- Family
- Work
- Team
- School
- Friends
- Other
- Me

HERstory | 49

Writing Workshop Part Two

Those You Are Closest To

Friends

1. What kind of qualities do you look for in a friend? What makes someone not just a friend but a best friend?

2. What are your favorite things to do when you hang out with your friends?

3. Have you ever been betrayed by a friend? How did it feel? How did you handle it?

4. Describe a time you were upset and a friend was there for you and helped you feel better.

5. Why do we need friends?

6. What are the most important things that your friends have taught you?

Family

1. What does it feel like to spend time around your family? What is it like being a preteen/teenage member of your family?

2. Who are the most important members of your family?

3. What is the best thing about your family?

4. What is one thing about your family that you wish could be different?

5. Why is it important to have family?

Mothers and Role Models

1. Name as many things as you can think of that you have learned from your mother.

2. In what ways are you similar to your mother? Do you look like your mother at all? In what ways?

3. In what ways are you different from your mother? Do you ever disagree with your mother? About what?

4. What kinds of dreams does your mother have for you?

5. Describe a favorite memory that you have of your mother.

6. If you could write your mother a letter thanking her for the things she has done for you, what would you say?

7. If you could write your mother a letter ten years from now telling her about the kind of woman you have become, what would you say?

8. What does it mean to be a role model? What makes someone a good role model?

9. Do you have a role model? Who? Why is this person your role model?

10. Are you a role model to anyone in your life?

11. Write shout-outs to two people who have helped you in your life.

12. Write R.I.P. shout-outs to two people whom you have loved and lost.

Movie Response Questions

The Sisterhood of the Traveling Pants

1. The four main characters have distinctly different personalities. Why do you think they are such close friends? What are the main ties that bind them?

2. Each of the girls is deeply affected by her relationship with her family. Can you think of some examples of how this is true? How has your relationship with your family shaped you?

3. Each of the girls must face a huge obstacle by the time the summer is over. How does facing these obstacles shape their character?

4. What do you think is the greatest gift that these girls give to one another through their friendship? What gifts do you give to those you love through your relationship with them?

5. In many ways these girls are one another's extended family. Do you have people you consider to be members of your family whom you are not related to by blood? What are the criteria to include someone in your "created family"?

6. How do you define the term "sisterhood"? How does this term apply to your experience in HERstory?

Body Intelligence

Take a few minutes to answer the following questions.

WHICH PART OR ASPECT OF MY BODY...

- is the strongest? _____
- is the weakest? _____
- is the most injury-prone? _____
- am I most comfortable with? _____
- am I least comfortable with? _____
- do other people notice first? _____
- do I really like but other people notice least? _____
- do I appreciate the most? _____

"IF YOU LIVED IN YOUR BODY, YOU'D BE HOME NOW."

Pretend you could move out of your body and someone new could move in. What tips would you give the new tenant about what it's like to live here? Consider the following:

What kind of care does this body need?

- Rest _____
- Feeding _____
- Watering _____
- Sunlight/Outdoors _____
- Physical Activity/Play _____
- Mental Stimulation _____
- Soothing/Peace _____
- Healing _____

- How do other people respond to this body?

- What tips can you pass on about how to manage this body?

- How does this body learn a new physical or mental skill? (Do you learn visually, audibly, through movement, etcetera?)

- Our bodies hear everything we think or say about ourselves. Take a moment to write a letter to your body. Tell it what you appreciate about it.

Dear _____,

Thank you for taking the time to listen to what I have to say. I appreciate you as much as you appreciate me!

With Love, _____

Body Appreciation

What has your body done for you lately?

- Fought off an infection
- Let you hear your favorite music
- Stayed awake so you could study for an exam
- Learned a new skill
- Rewarded you with the sight of a sunset
- Healed a bruise
- Let you enjoy a delicious meal
- Gotten stronger
- Enjoyed the wonderful smell of fresh flowers
- Kept working despite being in pain
- Expressed a strong emotion through your face and body language
- Defended you from an attack or healed from an attack
- Let you know through pain that something needed your attention
- Released you from pain
- Took a walk through the park
- Hugged someone you love
- Rejuvenated during sleep
- Danced all night long

Set aside some time each day to thank and appreciate the many capacities of your body.

Writing Workshop Part Three

Body Image

1. Do you think that young women in general have a positive body image? Why or why not?

2. Do you feel that you have a positive body image? Why or why not?

3. What messages do you think TV, movies, and magazines give young women about what their bodies should look like? About the way they dress?

4. What messages do you receive from your family about how you should look? From your friends?

5. What messages are young women given about going through puberty? How does going through puberty feel?

6. How do you feel about your body? Do you feel any pressure about having to look a certain way? Are you comfortable in your body? Why or why not?

7. Have you ever received a compliment related to how you look? An insult related to how you look? How did each one feel?

8. Have you ever insulted another girl about how she looks? Why do you think girls insult one another about their appearances?

9. List some compliments that women hear about their bodies and some insults that women hear about their bodies.

10. In the form of your own poem, what would you like to say to the world about the issue of young women's body image?

Movie Response Questions

Real Women Have Curves

1. In the movie, Anna receives a lot of different messages about her body. In general, there are a lot of messages aimed at women about their bodies. How do we know which ones to listen to?

2. What kind of culture did Anna grow up in? How do the expectations placed upon her affect the way people perceive her body? How does it affect the way she perceives her body?

3. Anna's parents do not believe that she should go to college but that instead she should work in the factory. What do you believe is right for Anna? How do we know what is right for us as individuals?

4. Have you ever wanted to show that you could exceed people's expectations? Explain.

5. Anna's actions in the garment factory inspire the women she works with to reveal the true nature of and celebrate their bodies. Why is it important for women to love and honor their bodies?

6. Anna stands up for how she believes women should be treated. What power do you have to set the tone for and create new traditions and expectations for the next generation of women?

Create Your Own Personals Ad

Create your own personals ad. Describe yourself. Be creative and specific. Don't lie! Spark the interest of your ideal match! Tell what your friends say are your award-winning qualities. Round out your profile with interesting information that highlights your unique personality, background, and interests. Go beyond the ordinary and offer up details. Keep in mind the compliments that were made about you during the Spin the Bottle game.

I am a _____, and I am _____ years old. I live in _____
_____.
I can describe my personality as _____.
I feel I am unique because _____
For fun I like to _____
_____.
My favorite way to spend my time is _____.
I am not interested in _____
Some of the goals I want to achieve are _____,
_____,
and _____.
When I think of the places I want to visit, _____ comes to mind.
Love means _____
_____
_____.
When I think of friendship, I think of _____
_____

To be totally honest, I want _____
_____.
I often dream of _____
I feel life is _____.
My friends often describe me as _____
_____
Some of the things I have to offer in a relationship are _____
_____
_____

Rate Your Mate

Have you ever imagined the person you might want to share your life with? Think of your *ideal* mate. Number the qualities below from 1 to 17: Number 1 means the quality is most important and number 17 means this quality is unimportant. Remember to use a different number for each!

_____ You share the same interests and enjoy doing things together.

_____ You get along with each other's families.

_____ You have the same friends.

_____ You find her/him physically attractive.

_____ He/She has money.

_____ You have similar personalities.

_____ You feel a passionate love for each other.

_____ You have similar goals and hopes for the future.

_____ He/She is a good communicator.

_____ Your desires about children and raising a family are the same.

_____ You share the same values and ethics.

_____ You both enjoy the same foods.

_____ He/She makes you laugh.

_____ You are friends first.

_____ You share the same religious beliefs.

_____ You are of the same race and cultural background.

_____ Fill in your own quality _____

Writing Workshop Part Four

Love and Relationships

Questions for Everyone

1. What does it feel like to have a crush?

2. Have you ever been in love? How does it feel?

3. Have you ever had your heart broken or gone through a breakup? How does/did it feel?

4. What makes someone attractive to you?

5. If you have an ex, is there anything you would still like to say to that person? Write it down.

6. Have you ever had a conflict with one of your friends over someone you were both interested in? What was that like?

7. How would you describe a first kiss?

8. How are young women treated in relationships? How should they be treated? How do you want to be treated in a relationship?

9. Write a love poem in any form that you wish. Allow your words to flow freely.

10. Is it easy or hard to trust someone in a relationship? Why?

11. Are there certain perceptions about how men should conduct themselves in a relationship? Are the perceptions about how women should conduct themselves different from those for men?

Movie Response Questions

Enchanted

1. Giselle's world morphed from one distinct reality to another. Do you ever feel like your reality is constantly changing?

2. Giselle was a very trusting character who was dedicated to her quest for love. What does trust have to do with love?

3. In the film, the expression of love is depicted in many different forms. If you had to demonstrate love as actions without words, what would those actions be?

4. In the film, Robert and Nancy learned that the best way to love each other was to let each other go. How do we know when to hold on and when to let go?

5. The plot of this movie offers a modern twist on the typical fairy-tale structure. For example, Giselle rescues Robert in the end instead of the typical "knight rescuing the maiden" scenario. How do you think women's roles in relationships have changed since your parents' time? What do you think the most important role of a woman in a relationship should be?

6. If you could write a modern fairy-tale ending to your own love story, what would it be?

For Just One Day

I would like to be _____
for just one day because . . .   (name of person from history)

I would like to be _____
for just one day because . . .   (name of celebrity)

I would like to be _____
for just one day because . . .   (name of fictional character)

Great Expectations!

I dream of . . .	What I envision happening and how I feel . . .	And it looks like . . .
Example: Going to college	Getting accepted at a college of my choice. I feel proud, smart, and competent. I can do this!	A letter in the mail, and then a beautiful campus where I am walking with new friends whom I met on my way to a class I really like.
Example: Being a star athlete	I win an Olympic gold medal and I feel like I'm on top of the world! Strong and successful.	Me on the podium with the medal around my neck and my fist raised, hearing the national anthem being played.

Choose one of the dreams above. How were you able to identify this as one of your dreams? (Example: I think about it all the time.)

In column one, put a star next to the dream(s) that come from your heart and a check next to the dream(s) that were influenced by other people in your life.

HERstory | 75

Writing Workshop Part Five

Dreams

1. What kind of dreams do you have for your future? What do you think you would like to be when you grow up?

2. Imagine yourself at age twenty-five. Where are you? What are you doing? Who are you with?

3. Do you think your dreams will come true? Why or why not?

4. What do you need to accomplish your dreams?

5. Who inspires you to keep chasing your dreams?

6. What kind of life do you dream about having?

7. What dreams does your family have for you?

8. Write a poem about what it feels like to have and chase a dream.

Movie Response Questions

Take the Lead

1. In this movie, the students have to take a leap of faith to trust Mr. Dulaine and follow his methods. When was a time that you had to take a leap of faith? What were the results?

2. In the movie, several characters face choices that will affect the course of their lives. Have you ever made a choice to follow one dream over another? Explain.

3. How can learning about someone's dreams help you better understand that person?

4. Have you ever been in a situation where your dreams were in direct conflict with someone else's? How can you resolve this type of situation?

5. Mr. Dulaine helped his students and in the process appeared to help himself. How can helping other people achieve their dreams affect your own dreams?

6. In one of the movie scenes, Rock notices LaRhette smiling to herself with her eyes closed as she dances, and when he asks her why, she responds, "Because it's my moment." What does your moment look like? What does it feel like?

Around My Way

Take a moment to think about where you are from, where you live, and even the block you live on, and how all these places influence the person you are. Now answer the following questions.

1. How has living in this country influenced who you are?

2. If your family is from another country or if you have ever lived in another country, how has that influenced who you are?

3. What town do you live in?

4. How has this town influenced who you are?

5. What neighborhood do you live in?

6. How has this neighborhood influenced who you are?

7. What block do you live on?

8. How has your block influenced who you are?

9. Which one of these influences you the most? Why?

10. Which one of these influences you the least? Why?

Show Your Pride

Create a slogan for a T-shirt that represents your heritage or tradition.

Example: "New York: What Dreams Are Made Of"

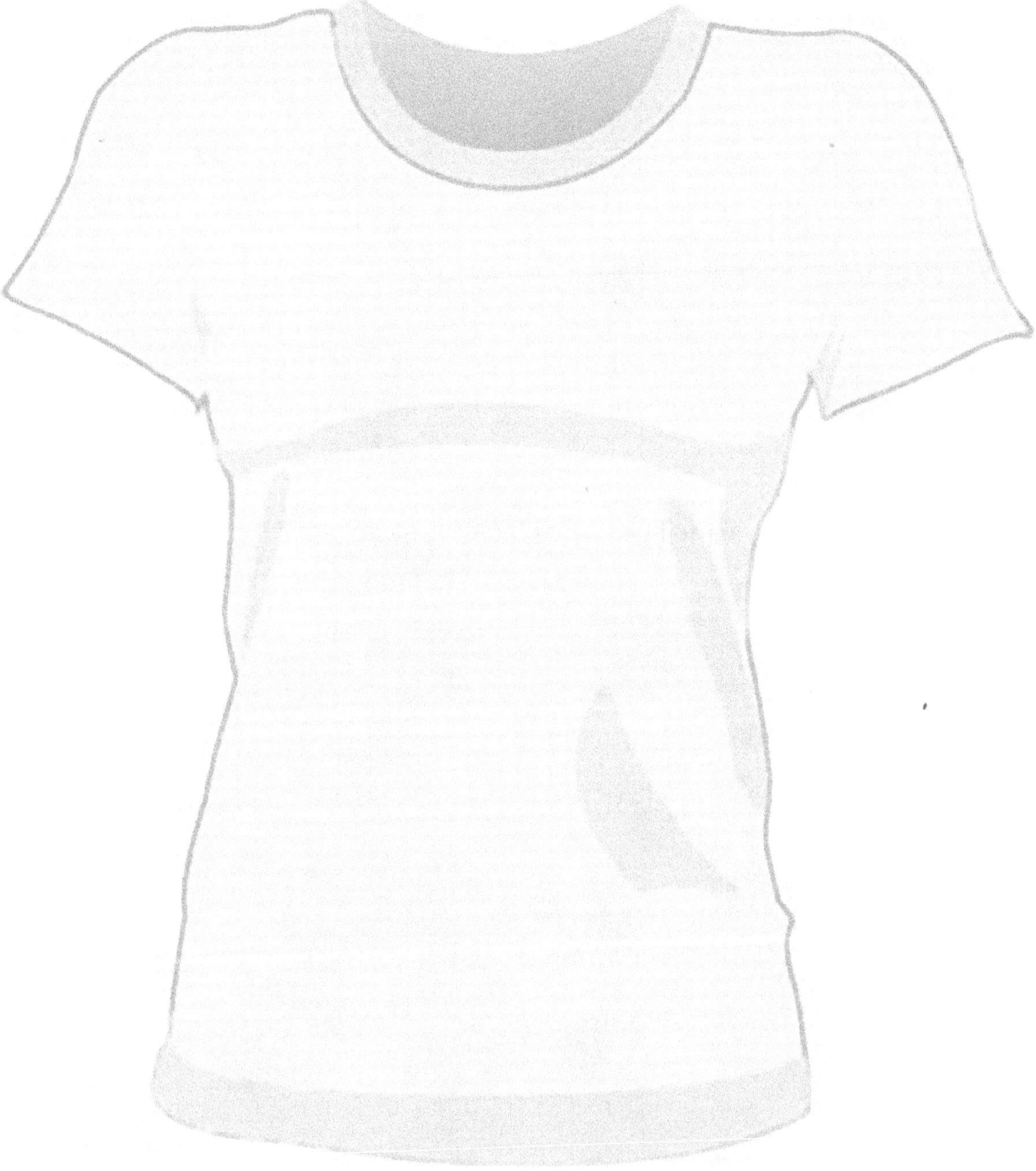

Writing Workshop Part Six

Heritage or Tradition

1. What are you most proud of about your heritage or tradition? What are you most proud of about where you and your family or your ancestors are from?

2. Describe your favorite part of the country that you consider yourself to be from.

3. Describe some of your favorite food or recipes handed down from your family or ancestors.

4. Describe some of your favorite rituals (e.g., holidays) that your ancestors or family of origin traditionally celebrate.

5. How are women treated in your family or cultural heritage? What is a woman's role? How do you feel about that?

6. If you or your family are not from the local area, are there any differences between the way women act where you are from and the way women act where you live now?

7. Does your heritage affect who you are? How?

8. What would you like to teach people about your heritage or your family?

I Am from . . . Poem

Answer the following prompts thoroughly:

- Where were you born?

- What is your family's heritage or tradition?

- Name two members of your family, living or deceased, whom you admire and why.

- Describe a family tradition.

- Describe two family customs.

- Describe a favorite family story.

- What is the first street address you remember from your childhood?

- Describe a household item, and name two household item brands.

- Describe a favorite part of your home using three sensory details.

- Name some favorite toys from your childhood.

- Name some favorite articles of clothing from your childhood.

- Name some favorite foods someone in your family made on special occasions, as well as who made them.

- Name some favorite games you played as a child.

- Name a secret place you liked to go to as a child.

- What is something an adult has said to you to encourage or praise you?

- What are some titles or lyrics from your favorite songs as a teenager?

- Name some heroes from history or literature.

- What is a dream you have for yourself?

Final I Am from . . . Poem

I am from _____. From _____ and from _____. I am from _____.

I am from _____, from _____, and _____. I am from _____. I am from _____. From _____ and from _____. Etcetera.

Movie Response Questions

The Great Debaters

1. The debate team students were from the same community and yet had very different perspectives about where they were from. How does the way we are raised affect how we view our heritage or tradition?

2. What does the term "heritage" mean to you? What does "tradition" mean? How about "blood," "ethnicity," "family," and "community"?

3. Are the students of Wiley College proud of their heritage? What does it mean to be proud of your heritage or tradition?

4. Have you ever been in a situation where you were judged as different because of your heritage or traditions? How did you react?

5. What is the best way to educate people about your heritage or tradition?

6. Samantha Booke is a groundbreaking character because she is the first female member of the debate team. Do you think young women today can consider trailblazing women such as Samantha part of their heritage? How have the women before us set the stage for us to succeed today?

Imagine

Please answer the following questions from the point of view of the character you are creating:

1. What is your name?

2. Where do you live (city and state/country)?

3. What is your job/career title?

4. How long have you worked in this industry or field?

5. What does "success" mean to you?

6. What did you do in high school that contributed to your success?

7. How did academic achievement in high school help you to become successful?

8. Why do you think you are successful?

9. What advice would you give to high school students who want to be successful in the future?

The Road Not Taken

By Robert Frost

Two roads diverged in a yellow wood,
And sorry I could not travel both
And be one traveler, long I stood
And looked down one as far as I could
To where it bent in the undergrowth;

Then took the other, as just as fair,
And having perhaps the better claim,
Because it was grassy and wanted wear;
Though as for that the passing there
Had worn them really about the same,

And both that morning equally lay
In leaves no step had trodden black.
Oh, I kept the first for another day!
Yet knowing how way leads on to way,
I doubted if I should ever come back.

I shall be telling this with a sigh
Somewhere ages and ages hence:
Two roads diverged in a wood, and I—
I took the one less traveled by,
And that has made all the difference.

Map of Your Dreams

HERstory | 93

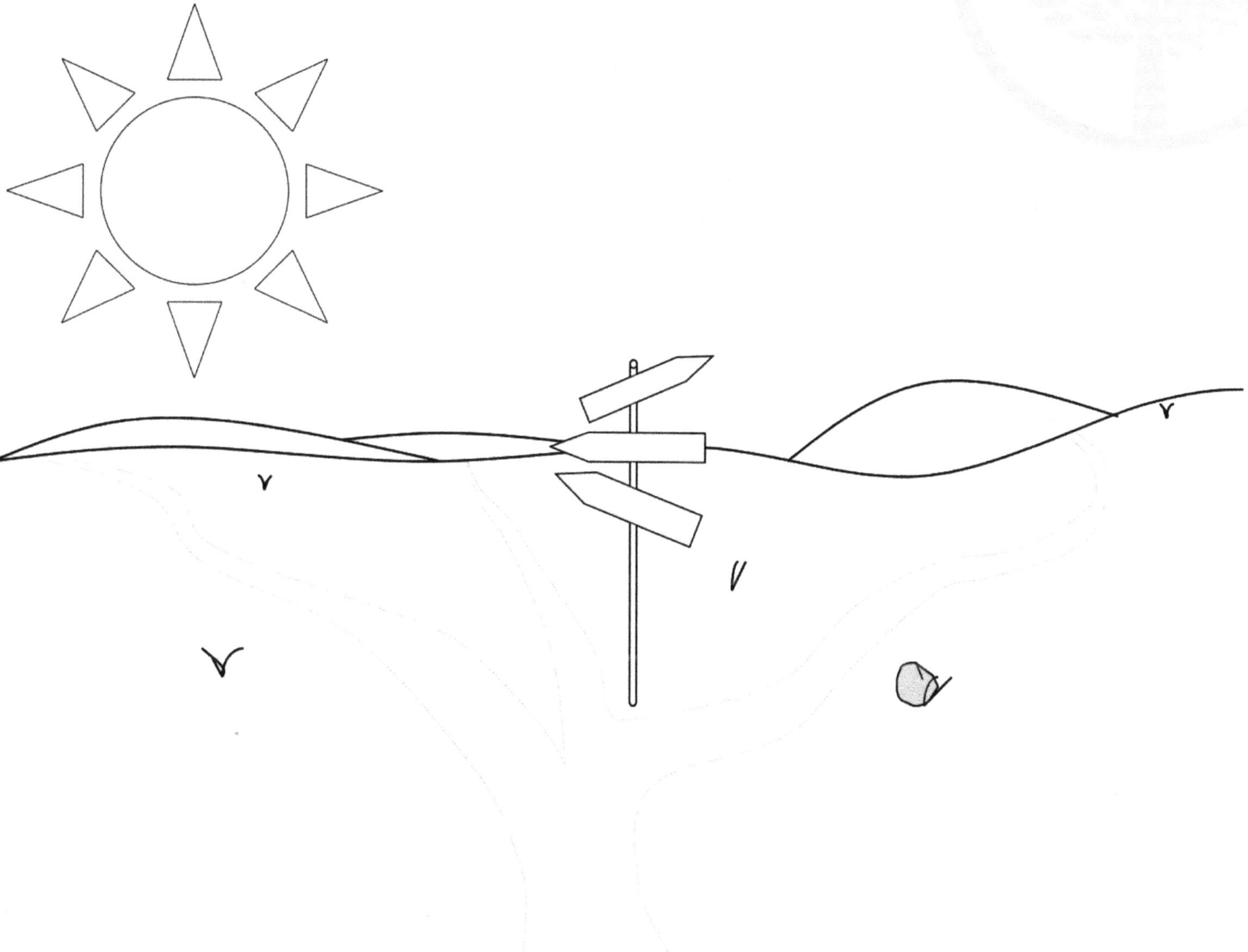

Writing Workshop Part Seven

Legacy

1. Describe something about the world around you that you would like to improve and explain why. Tell how improving it would affect the world.

2. If you became famous tomorrow, what is something that you would like the world to know about the real you?

3. After you have lived a full life, what do you think will be the three things that you will want the world to remember about you?

4. Write a letter to your future granddaughter telling her in detail about the most important lessons that you have learned about being a woman in this world.

5. What does the word "legend" mean to you? What is a personal legend?

6. Tell the story of why the world has never been the same since you came into it. What makes you unique? What can you contribute/give to the world that nobody else can?

7. Why is it so important for young women to have a voice?

8. What does it feel like for a young woman like you to free her voice?

Movie Response Questions

Pay It Forward

1. What values do you think Trevor stood for? What values do you stand for?

2. What do you think Trevor will be remembered for? What do you want to be remembered for?

3. Trevor created a movement that left a legacy that will affect the world long after his passing. What was the key element of his legacy?

4. How would you describe the concept of "pay it forward"? What effects do you think a movement like this would have on your community?

5. Do you think it is important to create change in the world? Explain.

6. Chris Chandler reported on the Pay It Forward movement that Trevor started, and thus his legacy only grew. Why is it important to learn about the legacy of those who came before us?

Creative Output

3

"Creativity takes courage."
— Henri Matisse

"Theatre was created to tell the truth about life."
— Anonymous

Group Poem

Collage Poem

THE ART OF WORDS GUIDE

Identity

My Reflection Drawing

Create a drawing of yourself that focuses on your internal qualities. This drawing will include your portrait and its reflection. Make the portrait show how you think others see you and the reflection show how you would like to be seen. The reflection can be in a mirror, a window, a puddle, etcetera. Use your imagination to envision where you might see the reflection of the "you" you want to be.

My Reflection Drawing

THE ART OF WORDS GUIDE
Those You Are Closest To

My Created Family Crest Drawing

Think about the people who make up your real or created family and those people who are closest to you. Consider what they mean to you and what each represents in your life. Design a coat of arms, crest, logo, or symbol that represents the people and symbols they've created. Include figures or words to show what the people in this family mean to you and how they are connected to you.

For the finished project, you may choose to draw the crest or coat of arms on a large scale that fills the paper and finish it either in color or black and white. Alternatively, you may use your imagination to incorporate the crest or coat of arms into a more detailed drawing (e.g., sketch the logo on a baseball cap, the medallion on a necklace or as part of the design of a piece of clothing that you are wearing).

My Created Family Crest Drawing

THE ART OF WORDS GUIDE
Body Image

My Body Is a Plant Collage or Drawing

Imagine that you have been asked to go to a greenhouse where houseplants and flowers are sold. At this greenhouse you can find any kind of plant, even imagine new plants—for example, a rose/cactus hybrid that smells like a gardenia. Pick out one plant in the greenhouse that represents your body. Draw that plant or create a colored construction-paper collage of it. Design this plant to showcase all that you like about your body. You may include words in the design of the plant as well. Think of the qualities of your body and try to give your plant some of those qualities. For example, if you like that you are strong, then you can design a strong and sturdy stem for your plant.

Next, refer to what you wrote in your body image writing worksheets and what you wrote on them. Now draw a tag for the plant that you just created. The tag can be hanging off the plant or sticking out of the ground near the plant. Ensure that the tag is large enough to fit care instructions for your body, referenced from the Body Intelligence worksheet. Your tag will include instructions such as: How often does it need to rest? How often does it need nurturing? What types of foods make it feel good? Does it need respect? Acceptance? Love?

My Body Is a Plant Collage or Drawing

THE ART OF WORDS GUIDE
Love and Relationships

The Heart of a Healthy Relationship Collage

Start by drawing a large heart on a piece of construction paper and cutting it out. Using magazines and pictures of your own friends and family, look for images that represent what you believe a healthy relationship looks like. You can also draw images and incorporate written words, if you prefer. Now collage the interior of the heart with the photographs, cutouts, drawings, words, etcetera.

Next, draw or use construction paper to cut out long twisting lengths of paper to create veins and arteries leading to the heart. Think of all the things that feed a healthy relationship, and fill those veins with words or symbols to represent them (e.g., trust, patience, understanding, fun). Instead of using words, you can use symbols to represent your ideas.

Your heart will now be surrounded by the representation of the vital elements of sustaining a healthy relationship.

The Heart of a Healthy Relationship Collage

THE ART OF WORDS GUIDE
Dreams

Outside My Window Drawing

Look at your list of five things you wish to accomplish in the future. Create a drawing that represents the inside of your room and that reflects your character and personality. Draw a dreamlike world outside the window or through a large hole in the wall or the ceiling of the room. In the world outside, create symbols for the five things you wish to accomplish. Use your imagination to find your own unique way to distinguish between the two worlds. For example, you might distinguish between the two worlds by playing with colors, juxtaposing black and white with color, or full color with a limited palette. Your choices should express who you are and your dreams.

Outside My Window Drawing

THE ART OF WORDS GUIDE
Heritage or Tradition

Delivery from an Ancestor Drawing

Imagine that you have a dream in which one of your ancestors visits you and hands you a very large container. What does the container look like? What materials is it made of? Does it have anything written on it? Draw this container in an open position so that you can see what is inside it. In it, draw the symbols, words, or literal representations of your family's heritage or tradition that have most affected who you are. Examples could include things that represent language, values, customs, etcetera. Remember this represents a dream, so let your imagination go wild.

Delivery from an Ancestor Drawing

THE ART OF WORDS GUIDE
Legacy

My Print, My Mark, My Legacy Drawing

Make a list of ten positive things that you bring to this world—for example: laughter, generosity, a good example for your little brother, love.

Then look very closely at your thumb to discern the shape of your thumbprint. Use the template provided on the following page. Complete the drawing by taking your list of ten things and using the words over the lightly sketched swirling lines of the thumbprint. You are thus using your words in the design of your thumbprint to compose a representation of what you believe will be your mark on the world.

My Print, My Mark, My Legacy Drawing

Say More: Journal Exercise

1. *Write about your experience in the acting lessons.*

2. What are some of your feelings and thoughts about performing?

Credits

Page 1 Ani DiFranco quote used with permission courtesy of Righteous Babe Records.

Page 33 Meg Rosoff quote used with permission courtesy of copyright owner Guardian News & Media Ltd.

About The Leadership Program

Our Vision

We create experiences that inspire people to step into their leadership and make positive change in their lives and in the world.

Who We Are

For over twenty years, The Leadership Program has worked to provide youth development activities and parent and professional development workshops and coaching.

The Leadership Program believes that with the right help, every person has the innate ability to lead the change.

For more information about Leadership Program publications and programs, visit our website at http://theleadershipprogram.com or contact us at info@tlpnyc.com.

Other program curriculum support available from The Leadership Program at www.tlpnyc.com/leadership-marketplace.

HERstory: Curriculum Suite

Boys 2 MENtors: Curriculum Manual

Boys 2 MENtors: Student Workbook

Empowering Upstanders: A School-Based Bullying Prevention Program

Empowering Upstanders: Student Workbook

Leadership Skills: High School Manual: Violence Prevention Project

Leadership Skills: High School Workbook: Violence Prevention Project

Leadership Skills: Middle School Workbook: Violence Prevention Project

Leadership Skills: Middle School Manual: Violence Prevention Project

www.ingramcontent.com/pod-product-compliance
Lightning Source LLC
Chambersburg PA
CBHW081840170426
43199CB00017B/2799